Peer Pressure
& Relationships

Bully on Campus & Online

Drugs & Alcohol

Gunman on Campus

Natural Disasters

Navigating Cyberspace

Peer Pressure & Relationships

Protecting Your Body: Germs, Superbugs, Poison, & Deadly Diseases

Road Safety

Sports

Stranger Danger

Terrorism & Perceived Terrorism Threats

Peer Pressure
& Relationships

Christie Marlowe

Mason Crest

Mason Crest
450 Parkway Drive, Suite D
Broomall, PA 19008
www.masoncrest.com

Printed and bound in the United States of America.

First printing
9 8 7 6 5 4 3 2 1

Series ISBN: 978-1-4222-3044-2
ISBN: 978-1-4222-3050-3
ebook ISBN: 978-1-4222-8834-4

Library of Congress Cataloging-in-Publication Data

Marlowe, Christie.
  Peer pressure & relationships / Christie Marlowe.
     pages cm. – (Safety first)
  Includes index.
  Audience: Ages 10+
  Audience: Grade 4 to 6.
  ISBN 978-1-4222-3050-3 (hardback)—ISBN 978-1-4222-3044-2 (series)—ISBN 978-1-4222-8834-4 (ebook) 1. Peer pressure in adolescence–Juvenile literature. 2. Peer pressure–Juvenile literature. 3. Interpersonal relations–Juvenile literature. I. Title.
  HQ799.2.P44M37 2015
  303.3'27–dc23
                                        2014003851

Contents

Introduction

No task is more important than creating safe schools for all children. It should not require an act of courage for parents to send their children to school nor for children to come to school. As adults, we must do everything reasonable to provide a school climate that is safe, secure, and welcoming—an environment where learning can flourish. The educational effectiveness and the strength of any nation is dependent upon a strong and effective educational system that empowers and prepares young people for meaningful and purposeful lives that will promote economic competitiveness, national defense, and quality of life.

Clearly adults are charged with the vital responsibility of creating a positive educational climate. However, the success of young people is also affected by their own participation. The purpose of this series of books is to articulate what young adults can do to ensure their own safety, while at the same time educating them as to the steps that educators, parents, and communities are taking to create and maintain safe schools. Each book in the series gives young people tools that will empower them as participants in this process. The result is a model where students have the information they need to work alongside parents, educators, and community leaders to tackle the safety challenges that face young people every day.

Perhaps one of the most enduring and yet underrated challenges facing young adults is bullying. Ask parents if they can remember the schoolyard bully from when they were in school, and the answers are quite revealing. Unfortunately, the situation is no better today—and new venues for bullying exist in the twenty-first-century world that never existed before. A single bully can intimidate not only a single student but an entire classroom, an entire school, and even an entire community. The problem is underscored by research from the National School Safety Center and the United States Secret Service that indicates that bullying was involved in 80 percent of school shootings over the past two decades. The title in this series that addresses this problem is a valuable and essential tool for promoting safety and stopping bullying.

Another problem that has been highlighted by the media is the threat of violence on our school campuses. In reality, research tells us that schools are the safest place for young people to be. After an incident like Columbine or Sandy Hook, however, it is difficult for the public, including students, to understand that a youngster is a hundred times more likely to be assaulted or killed at home or in the community than at school. Students cannot help but absorb the fears that are so prevalent in our society. Therefore, a frank, realistic, discussion of this topic, one that avoids hysteria and exaggeration, is essential for our young people. This series offers a title on this topic that does exactly that. It addresses questions such as: How do you deal with a gunman on the campus? Should you run, hide, or confront? We do not want to scare our children; instead, we want to empower them and reassure them as we prepare them for such a crisis. The book also covers the changing laws and school policies that are being put in place to ensure that students are even safer from the threat of violence in the school.

"Stranger danger" is another safety threat that receives a great deal of attention in the modern world. Again, the goal should be to empower rather than terrify our children. The book in this series focusing on this topic provides young readers with the essential information that will help them be "safety smart," not only at school but also between home and school, at play, and even when they are home alone.

Alcohol and drug abuse is another danger that looms over our young people. As many as 10 percent of American high school students are alcoholics. Meanwhile, when one student was asked, "Is there a drug problem in your school?" her reply was, "No, I can get all the drugs I want." A book in this series focuses on this topic, giving young readers the information they need to truly comprehend that drugs and alcohol are major threats to their safety and well-being.

From peer pressure to natural disasters, from road dangers to sports safety, the Safety First series covers a wide range of other modern concerns. Keeping children and our schools safe is not an isolated challenge. It will require all of us working together to create a climate where young people can have safe access to the educational opportunities that will promote the success of all children as they transition into becoming responsible citizens. This series is an essential tool for classrooms, libraries, guidance counselors, and community centers as they face this challenge.

Dr. Ronald Stephens
Executive Director
National School Safety Center
www.schoolsafety.us

Words to Know

traumatic: Emotionally troubling or damaging.
apprehension: Worry or fear that holds you back from doing something.
anxiety: A worried or nervous feeling, often to do with something that hasn't happened yet.

Chapter One

Real-Life Stories

We've all wanted to fit in with a group of people. Maybe you've moved to a new town, and you want to make new friends. Or maybe you want to be part of the "cool" group at school. Or you just started playing on a sports team, and you want to prove you're a good athlete.

Many people have felt the need to fit in. That need is sometimes called peer pressure. Wanting to fit in is natural. No one wants to feel left out all the time. But sometimes wanting to fit in can make you act in ways you don't really want. You may do something dangerous or something you're uncomfortable doing just to fit in.

Peer pressure makes you do something you normally wouldn't do to be part of a group. Your peers are the people around you who are most like you. They're your "group." They are usually your own age. You go to school with them. And you probably spend time with them outside school.

One young woman shared her story online on a site called Eduguide (www.eduguide.org). She says, "In eighth grade, I became best friends with this girl named Jenny. She seemed like she would be a very good friend. I guess that's when I learned that you should never judge a book by its cover.

"I soon learned that she was the exact opposite of a good friend. She would put me down, say mean things about me to other people, and toward the end of our friendship, she would go out

9

It can be very hard to say no to something your friends are asking you to do—but if you know it's unhealthy or wrong, you should still do what's best for you.

Peer Pressure & Relationships

with the guys that I liked. I would tell myself that she was just having a bad day, or that I was just imagining things.

"We did have a lot of fun together, although, through teenage peer pressure, I mostly got in trouble with her. Every day my self-esteem would be lowered in some way by her."

Even though her friend was mean, the girl telling this story still wanted Jenny to like her. She started doing unhealthy things because of Jenny. She says, "Jenny would tell me that I looked like a hippo in my clothes and that I needed to lose a lot of weight because I was fat. She would try and get me to starve myself.

"She got mad when I wouldn't listen to her, so finally I just gave up and did what she wanted because I wanted my best friend to be happy. I only managed to starve myself for a week.

"Starving yourself is very unhealthy; it causes you a lot of problems. Jenny ended up in the hospital after two months of starving herself. She couldn't smell food without getting sick. You should never give in to what your friends tell you to do if there's any doubt in your mind that it can hurt you or that it's wrong."

This girl realized she was doing things she shouldn't be doing because of her friend. "Eventually I stopped hanging out with her so much," she explains. "I would only talk to her about once a month, if that. My self-esteem was gradually increasing. I started hanging out with better friends. I was doing well."

This young woman learned her lesson. She tells other young people, "You should never be friends with someone that is going to put you down all the time! If this or something similar is going on with you, ask yourself: is it worth feeling bad about yourself just to be friends with someone who doesn't deserve your friendship?"

Lauren also got in trouble when she was younger because of what other people made her do. Her story, which she told on Intervene.Drugfree.org, is a little different from the story we just heard.

She says, "As a young girl, two of the more **traumatic** things I went through were growing up with an alcoholic parent and my parents' divorce. I tried to stuff the void I experienced with drugs and alcohol. . . .

"I was starved for attention as a kid, and I didn't have the coping skills I needed to go through the kinds of things the adults around me were putting me through. I became a great actress, with the ability to mold myself into what others wanted me to be, a trait that came in handy once I started using [drugs] full time.

"The fact that I gave into peer pressure—big time—is no big surprise. Other people's solutions to what I was going through—no matter how much bad judgment was there—was an easy way to let myself off the hook for my own behavior.

"I wanted to fit in and feel better about myself. Because I didn't feel like I could turn to my parents for advice and guidance, I turned to my peers. As a teenager who was already full of **apprehension** and **anxiety**, getting caught up and swept away by peer pressure was just another high.

"Stealing alcohol from the local grocery store seems like a good idea until the cops show up and you're busted. As a teen, I had a hard time grasping that my own judgment was impaired. I kept making bad decisions because I desperately wanted to belong and be accepted.

Real-Life Stories

11

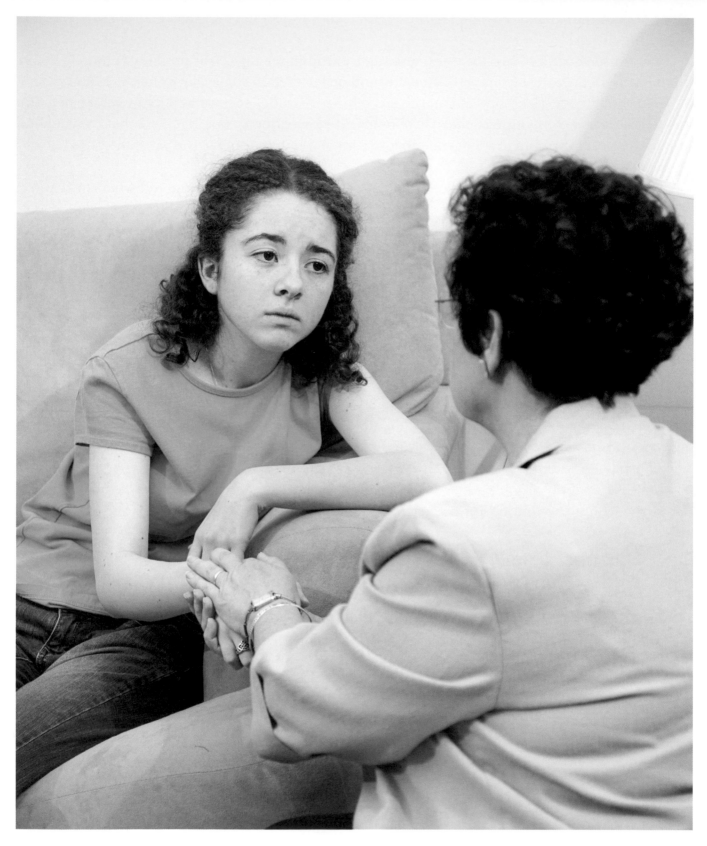

Don't be afraid to get help if you're in trouble! There are many people who are trained to know exactly how to help you through tough situations.

12

Peer Pressure & Relationships

At first, alcohol might make you feel good, but that feeling won't last forever and using alcohol can end up hurting you.

"At first, drugs and alcohol gave me confidence, self-esteem, and filled that void I'd carried around with me for so many years."

Lauren didn't think twice about doing the drugs. After all, everyone around her used them. "Peer pressure is something all teens live with. Teenagers spend most of their waking hours with their peers—not their family members."

But then she got help. Lauren went to drug rehab to get sober and stop using drugs. While she was there, she met lots of people who influenced her in a good way. She says, "It was only when I finally got checked into a treatment center that worked with adolescent substance abuse that I found myself a whole new set of peers who were working towards the same goals as I was. It was easier to stay sober when I surrounded myself with other sober teens.

Try to surround yourself with people who encourage you to make healthy choices. When your friends are being responsible, you'll want to be, too!

Peer Pressure & Relationships

Can Peer Pressure Ever Be a Good Thing?

Most of the time when people talk about peer pressure, they're talking about bad behavior. Peer pressure is the reason many young people bully others, have sex, do drugs, join gangs, or commit crimes. Peer pressure doesn't necessarily mean you're being pushed to act in a bad way, though. Sometimes it can be good. If everyone around you eats vegetables, and you're the only one who doesn't, you'll feel left out. You'll start eating vegetables to fit in, which is a good thing for your health! In this chapter, Lauren was peer pressured to stop doing drugs. Fitting in with a group of healthy, positive people can be very good for us. But fitting in for the wrong reasons or with a negative group of people can also be very dangerous!

"The chances of staying sober were slim to none had I gone back to my old friends and hangouts. The pressure and feelings of 'missing out' would have been too much for me to handle." Lauren found a way out.

Both of these young people dealt with peer pressure. Although they did things that made them uncomfortable, eventually they figured out how to stay true to themselves. Other young people can use their stories to beat peer pressure in their lives. So in a way, they've turned the picture around—now they're helping to contribute to positive peer pressure.

Words to Know

confident: Feeling good about yourself.
cliques: Small groups of people who get along with each other but may keep others out of the group.

Chapter Two

What Makes Peer Pressure Dangerous?

Peer pressure can make young people (and adults) act differently from how they normally would. The desire to fit in is very powerful. It can make us willing to do all sorts of things. When it comes to staying safe, your best bet is to not listen to peer pressure. Your friends may not always want what is best for you. Knowing what is best for you is the first step in avoiding bad influences and staying safe.

PEER PRESSURE AND BULLYING

Some young people become bullies so that other people will accept them. Someone who picks on others is a bully. They may get their friends to bully people, too.

People become bullies for different reasons. They may think, *If everyone else bullies this person, that means I have to.* Or, *If I don't bully someone else, my friends might bully me.*

Some kids bully others to impress friends. Others bully because they want attention from their peers, parents, or teachers. It doesn't matter if it is attention for doing something they shouldn't. They just want others to pay attention to them.

Bullies might not know how to handle their anger or function well in life, so they're more likely to end up committing violent crimes.

Peer Pressure & Relationships

The Effects of Bullying

Bullies have existed for a long time. And all those bullies have caused some big problems! Bullying can have some very dangerous effects on both the bully and the person being bullied. According to StopBullying.gov, a person being bullied may feel a lot of sadness and loneliness, have more health problems, and have more trouble with his schoolwork. Those being bullied sometimes even turn to violence and push back against bullies and others. Young people doing the bullying are affected as well. Many of them don't know how to deal with bad feelings and turn to bullying to let out those feelings. Bullies are more likely to abuse drugs, commit violent crimes, drop out of school, and be violent later in life.

Some young people bully others with words. They make fun of and tease others. Other bullies are violent. They start fights and encourage their friends to join in.

Bullies often appear **confident**. A bully may seem to think he's the greatest person in the world. He is so confident, he can put other people down. But it's probably all an act. Many bullies have very little confidence in themselves. They may even not like themselves very much. They try to feel better about themselves by putting other people down.

A lack of confidence like this is a sign of low self-esteem. Someone's self-esteem is a measure of how much a person values herself. Many young people have low self-esteem. And many people with low self-esteem think they only have value if their peers accept them.

If you sometimes don't feel good about yourself, it's normal. But you should try to turn around that low self-esteem. Have positive thoughts about yourself. Don't let feeling bad about yourself turn into bullying other people. And don't let low self-esteem make you give in to peer pressure to bully others.

PEER PRESSURE AND DRUG USE

Whenever you hear about peer pressure, you'll probably also hear about drugs. One of the most common things young people do because of peer pressure is take drugs. Some are under pressure to smoke cigarettes or drink alcohol to fit in. These are drugs, too.

People use drugs for many reasons. Some people use drugs to avoid problems they have in life. They don't want to think about their problems, so they take drugs. They think the drugs will make them feel better.

Another of the most common reasons young people take drugs is to be "cool." They feel like everyone is doing it, so they should, too. They think to be normal and fun, they have to take drugs.

Most young people feel peer pressure to do drugs, drink alcohol, and smoke cigarettes at some point. Many of them give in.

Using drugs because other people want you to (or you think other people want you to) is dangerous. The risks of drug use are very real.

People who feel like they're unable to get respect in other ways might turn to a gang to get that respect through violence and crime.

Peer Pressure & Relationships

People who do drugs at an early age are more likely to have bad grades and drop out of school. They often don't learn how to deal with bad feelings. They never learn how to handle emotions in a healthy way.

And, of course, drugs are bad for your physical health. Depending on the drug, users can end up with loss of memory, upset stomachs, liver disease, cancer, and more.

Serious drug abuse can also lead to addiction. Addiction is when your body and mind need a drug to function. Addiction is a disease. It causes problems with friends, family, school, and jobs.

Drug users sometimes overdose. An overdose is when someone takes too much or too many drugs for her body to handle. An overdose can lead to severe physical damage or even death!

Scientists have proven a link between drugs like alcohol and nicotine (found in cigarettes) and cancer and other serious health conditions. People can die from these diseases, too.

Despite knowing these risks, many young people still give in to peer pressure to take drugs. It's hard to say no right now because of health risks in the future.

Drinking alcohol is one of the most common peer pressures for young people. It may seem like all your friends drink. You may feel if you don't drink, you won't fit in. You may be afraid your friends will stop hanging out with you. That's a lot of pressure to drink!

But not everyone drinks. Drinking when you're under twenty-one is illegal. Drinking too much is dangerous, too. Getting drunk makes you take risks you wouldn't otherwise take. And some teenagers drive while they're drunk, which is extremely dangerous.

People who know all that may still drink anyway. If you're hanging out with your friends, and everyone else is drinking, it's hard not to join in. You need to do what's right for you. Ask yourself: What will make me safe and happy in the long run?

VIOLENCE AND CRIME

Some people turn to violence and crime because of peer pressure. Maybe you think committing crimes will impress you peers. You may feel if you don't commit a crime, you won't fit in with a certain group of people. It might be something that seems little and harmless, like stealing some makeup from a drugstore or breaking and entering an empty house. What seems like something small, though, can lead to big legal problems that could change your future. And any time guns are involved, even if you never planned to use them, the chance of violence can lead to very, very big problems.

Gangs are another example. Gangs are groups of people with something in common who commit crimes together. Gangs are a little like **cliques** found in schools. But gangs tend to be violent. They may sell drugs, rob people, or even hurt and kill. Gangs are found in lots of cities around the United States. There are also some gangs outside cities.

Young people join gangs for many reasons. Gangs help people make money. They give people a group of friends that act almost like family. In some cases, gangs may be the only family someone knows. They protect people on the street from violence.

Kids and teens feel pressure to join a gang for various reasons. In some areas, almost every

Negative peer pressure can take many forms. Your friends might ask you to do many things that aren't good for you in the long run—like skipping school.

Peer Pressure & Relationships

What Is a Gang?

Not everyone agrees on exactly what a gang is. But the U.S. government has some guidelines it uses to set a gang apart from other kinds of organizations:

- A gang is a group of three or more people.
- A gang's members have a group identity meant to create fear or intimidation.
- A gang's purpose is partly to engage in crime.
- A gang's crime and violence is meant to increase the group's power and respect.

young person is in a gang. Sometimes, if someone doesn't join a gang, he faces more than just pressure; he faces violence. It's easier and safer to join a gang than to be alone on the streets.

Gang violence has its obvious risks. Thousands of young people get in serious trouble because of gang-related crimes each year. And some studies estimate that over ten thousand people a year die because of gang-related violence.

No matter the cost, young people still seek the acceptance of their peers. And others continue to try to impress those around them. Gangs are perhaps the most extreme example of peer pressure. But they also show just how truly dangerous peer pressure can be.

OTHER RISKY AND WRONG BEHAVIORS

Peer pressure can make you take all sorts of risks you wouldn't normally dare to do. Once you have several people telling you to do something, it's hard to say no.

In one recent study, scientists took a look at how teenagers drive. The study found teens are more likely to practice risky driving when two or three friends are in the car. These scientists concluded the risky driving was because teenager wanted to impress their friends and didn't care as much about driving safely.

Peer pressure makes kids do plenty of other risky or wrong things. Young people sometimes feel pressure to skip school. Say, for example, your friends think it would be cool to blow off school. They might pressure you to join them, even though you'd rather stay in class and learn. You don't want to get bad grades.

In another group, you might feel pressure to spend a lot of money. If your friends always buy expensive video games, clothes, jewelry, or other things, you'll think you should, too. Those people might even say you have to buy that stuff in order to hang out with them or be cool.

Peer pressure can be about anything—for example, stealing, cheating on tests, looking a certain way. If people are trying to make you do something you don't want to do—that's negative peer pressure. Luckily, there are ways to fight peer pressure and stay strong.

Words to Know

supportive: Encouraging and positive.
compassion: Understanding other people's feelings.

Chapter Three

Staying Safe and Being Prepared

Negative peer pressure is hard for us to fight. After all, most of us want to fit in. We want to be part of a group and have friends. We want to be accepted. All those feelings are totally normal. But we get in trouble when our need to be accepted makes us do things we don't really want to do.

In the past, people thought that if kids and teens were taught what would happen if they caved in to peer pressure, they would stop. In other words, if someone knew about the dangers of using drugs, she just wouldn't give in to the peer pressure.

Unfortunately, teaching people about the consequences of giving in to peer pressure isn't enough. Our desire to fit in is just too strong. It's stronger than the risks of negative peer pressure.

Now people are using different ways to fight against peer pressure. Adults and young people alike know the world will be a better place without so much negative peer pressure!

TEACHING ADULTS

Nobody grows up alone. We all have people who take care of us when we're young. These people help shape us in who we become.

The adults who take care of us when we're very little have a lot to do with how much peer pressure affects us. They also have much to do with our self-esteem, how much we value ourselves.

Adults who are **supportive** and make kids feel like they are good people have a good influence

25

Having positive adult role models in your life can help to prevent some of the negative effects that peer pressure might have.

Peer Pressure & Relationships

Parents can have more influence over their children than anyone else. If you have a happy, healthy family life, you're more likely to grow into a happy, healthy person.

on young people. People who have supportive adults in their young lives are more likely to say no to negative peer pressure and make good decisions. The opposite is true for young people who didn't have supportive adults when they were little.

So one of the best ways of fighting peer pressure is to deal with it before it even happens. If adults' relationships with their kids are healthier and better, young people will have an easier time not giving in to peer pressure.

Good relationships with adults help young people in other ways, too. Adults, especially family, can show little kids what good, healthy relationships look like. Once a kid knows what a healthy relationship is, she'll look for healthy relationships the rest of her life. She'll know that being friends with someone who peer pressures her isn't a healthy relationship. She'll know that person isn't really her friend.

Parents, teachers, and other adults can take advantage of many programs, books, and more about helping children avoid negative peer pressure. People are trying to teach adults how to be more supportive of their kids and help them build self-esteem. The more self-esteem children have, the more they'll avoid peer pressure!

CAMPAIGNS

If someone doesn't know why drinking too much is bad, he won't have any reason to stop. Teaching

Sometimes, the hardest part of saying no is the fear of disappointing your friends, but that doesn't mean that you should let them convince you to do something dangerous or unhealthy.

Peer Pressure & Relationships

Peer Pressure and the Brain

Science tells us how peer pressure works in our brains. Studies show teens take more risks when other teenagers are around. They saw the part of the brain that has to do with the good feelings of rewards were more actively involved when teens' friends were there to see them take risks. The brains of adults and kids didn't show as much activity in the same part of the brain. Most people consider the rewards and risks of an action before taking the action. But scientists now think that the teenage brain is more likely to ignore the risks of an action in favor of the rewards.

people *why* to say no to dangerous risks is another way we're fighting peer pressure. Peer-pressure campaigns are plans for giving young adults the information they need to make smart decisions.

Campaigns are often lots of advertisements all aimed at a goal. Anti-drug campaigns, for example, consist of advertisements on TV, radio, online, and on billboards meant to teach people to say no to drugs. Anti-bullying campaigns are advertisements that teach about bullying. Sometimes school programs are part of these campaigns. Schools and other community organizations can give teenagers important information for making wise choices.

Peer pressure takes place when young people don't know how to say no to their peers. They're afraid saying no will make them seem weak or uncool. A young person may completely understand the risks she is taking—but if she has low self-esteem, saying no can still be difficult. She doesn't know how to say no with confidence. Campaigns can give students the tools they need to stand up with confidence to negative peer pressure.

The Just Say No campaign took place back in the 1980s in the United States. This is an early example of a campaign designed to teach young people how to say no to drugs and alcohol without fear. It focused on teaching young people to simply say no with confidence. It taught young people they didn't have to explain their decision to stay away from drugs and alcohol. Saying no was enough.

More recent anti-gang and anti-bullying campaigns have followed the same path. These campaigns let young people know they have choices when it comes to joining gangs or bullying others.

Antigang campaigns usually take place in areas with a lot of gang violence. For example, some billboards in Salinas, California, fight youth violence. One billboard says, "Choose Your House." It has two pictures—one is a prison and the other is a comfortable family home. Another billboard says, "Choose Your Ceremony." This one has a picture of a funeral and a picture of a college graduation ceremony. The message is short but clear.

Billboards like these do two things. They remind young people they have a choice when it comes to joining a gang and committing crimes. They also clearly show what can happen when young people make the wrong decisions.

Anti-bullying campaigns do the same thing. They show young people they have a choice. They can bully, or they can choose not to bully. No one *has* to become a bully!

A recent commercial by the I Choose anti-bullying campaign begins by reminding young

Choose to be a positive force in your own life. If you have a good effect on those around you, you'll be surrounded by people who have a positive effect on you!

Peer Pressure & Relationships

Adult Peer Pressure

Peer pressure exists at every age. For adults, peer pressure is part of the reason they might decide to spend their money on really expensive things they don't need, worry about their appearance, or even choose to get married. Peer pressure for adults isn't very different from peer pressure at any other age. It can be both positive and negative. However, studies have shown that adults are generally better at understanding and avoiding risks. This may be because they have had time to see the consequences of their actions. They may still feel the need to impress their peers, but adults are generally better at stopping short of putting themselves in danger simply to gain respect or acceptance.

people that "Bullying is a choice," and, "The power to choose is yours." The young people in the commercial talk about their choices saying, "I choose friendship. I choose compassion. I choose respect. I choose kindness. I choose love." Commercials like these remind us that the pressure to bully may be strong but that it is still a choice.

The I Choose campaign has other ways to spread its message. You can buy an I Choose bracelet to show that you choose not to be a bully. You can read news articles about bullying and people's firsthand stories about their experiences with bullying. These show how horrible bullying is. In response, you can decide to make five anti-bullying choices: friendship, kindness, respect, **compassion**, and love. Teachers can also teach a program about bullying created by the campaign. The I Choose campaign is working!

Campaigns like these offer young people some of the tools they need to stand up to peer pressure in a positive way. But using these tools is up to you!

Words to Know

motivates: Drives or pushes.
blasé: Unimpressed or bored with.
statistics: Numbers that show important information.
restraint: Holding back.

Chapter Four

What Can You Do to Stay Safe?

Negative peer pressure is dangerous. It is also very difficult to stand up against. You can choose to stand up to peer pressure, though. There are plenty of things you can do to stay true to yourself and make the decisions you know are right.

KNOW YOUR CHOICES

The very first thing you should do is discover what choices you can make. Figure out what you're comfortable doing and what you don't want to do. If you know your choices, you'll be able to think more clearly the next time you're faced with peer pressure.

For example, you might decide ahead of time that you don't want to skip school. You know you want to go to class, learn, and get good grades, because someday you want to go to college and then get a good job. If you're clear about what your goals are, then if someone asks you to skip school with him, you'll know what to do. You already know you don't want to. So it's easier to say no.

You should also decide to be yourself. Part of the problem of peer pressure is that it sometimes makes you be someone you're not. Take time to be alone sometimes. Think about who you want to be. Think about what feels right to you. Don't become a different person just to make someone think you're cool.

It's important to be positive! If you have good self-esteem, you'll be more able to say no to decisions that you know aren't good.

Peer Pressure & Relationships

Don't be afraid to be unique. If you're true to yourself, you'll be happier and feel better about the choices that you make.

Part of deciding to be yourself is thinking good thoughts about yourself. Feeling good about themselves is hard for a lot of people. Most of us think about all the ways we fail—we're not cool enough, we don't have enough friends, we don't get good enough grades, we're not good enough at music or sports. Try thinking good things about yourself instead. Congratulate yourself when you get a good grade. Focus on how hard you try at music or sports, and how much better you've gotten. Think about all the people who love and care about you.

When you think good thoughts, you start to feel better about yourself. You feel better being yourself. You're happy being you. And that makes it a lot easier to be true to yourself and say no to peer pressure.

Have your own opinions about things. Work on a personal style that is all your own. Don't be afraid of being different. Some groups might not appreciate your differences. But you will find those that do!

What Can You Do to Stay Safe?

It's important to learn to say no confidently. If you do, then you can refuse to do things you don't want to do without making people pressure you—and you'll feel better about yourself.

Peer Pressure & Relationships

AVOID NEGATIVE PEER PRESSURE

If you stay away from negative peer pressure, you won't have to worry about fighting it. No one can completely avoid peer pressure. But you can choose to hang out with people who don't pressure you to do things you don't want to do. Take advantage of positive peer pressure. Choose friends who will help you form good habits and achieve your goals!

Recognize when someone you know is pressuring you. A true friend accepts it when you don't want to do something she wants to do. She lets you make your own decisions. Real friends don't make you do things that make you uncomfortable.

Stay away from people who are impressed when you do risky things. Taking drugs and committing crimes aren't things that should impress others. They are dangerous and against the law. They could get you in serious trouble and hurt your future. Choose friends who know that.

Really think about the people you hang out with. Do they make you feel uncomfortable all the time? Do they make you do things that you otherwise might not do? Do they make you feel bad if you refuse to do something they're doing? Or do they respect your boundaries and choices? Do they avoid pressuring you to do things you don't want to do? If a friend or a group of friends ever wants you to do something that could hurt yourself, others, or another person's property, start looking for other people to be around.

LEARN HOW TO SAY NO

No matter how hard you try to stay away from negative peer pressure, you'll still come across it once in a while. You'll find peer pressure when you least expect it. You should know how to deal with peer pressure whenever and wherever it happens.

Sometimes just walking away isn't an option. Situations like these can be uncomfortable, but learning how to confidently say no can save you from doing something you'll regret.

Imagine someone offers you a cigarette after school. You don't want to smoke, because you know it's not good for you. You have two choices—give in or say no.

Confidently saying, "No, thanks," is the first thing you should do. Let the people offering you a cigarette know right away that you don't want to smoke. They're more likely to leave you alone if you say no right away. If you say, "Maybe," or seem unsure, they'll think you might really want to smoke.

When a group of people does risky things, you are probably not the only one who feels uncomfortable. Someone else in the group might also be feeling uncomfortable. When you say no, you're giving other people the courage to say no, too.

Saying no once won't always work. The people or person pressuring you might not give up right away. You still have a few options left, though. Don't give in!

You can make an excuse. That's what parents are good for! If you don't want to go to a party where you know there will be drugs, for example, you can always blame your parents. "My parents won't let me." You can also simply say, "I am uncomfortable doing that." That may seem uncool,

You wouldn't want someone else to pressure you into doing something you don't want to do—make sure you treat others the same way.

Peer Pressure & Relationships

Adult Peer Pressure

Canada's National Anti-Drug Strategy website (*www.nationalantidrugstrategy.gc.ca*) has some tips on saying no to drugs. Check them out:

> I don't want to end up like that "has-been" celebrity.
> I'm not in the mood.
> I can't take a chance with my asthma (or bronchitis, or any other health problem that could be worsened by drug use).
> I don't have the time, I've already promised to meet (insert name).
> I'm already late for work.
> I have to be home soon and I can't risk getting into trouble for being late.
> Can you imagine what would happen if my parents found out? No way—I want to live until at least tomorrow.
> Nah—I'm good, thanks.
> I'll pass—I'm not into that stuff.
> I've got a long day tomorrow and don't want to feel awful.

Or, you can also choose from one of the following:

> Respect my decision—I respect yours.
> Look, I'd rather not.
> I'll catch up with you tomorrow—I've got other things I'd like to do.

but if you say it with confidence, others will usually leave you alone. If people put you down for acting on your values, they may not be the sort of people you want to be friends with anyway.

Sometimes you can just walk away. You don't have to be around people smoking after school. Just walk home, or get on the bus. Or pretend you left something inside. Getting away from the situation can help you stay strong.

DON'T PEER PRESSURE OTHERS

We've all heard the Golden Rule: treat others the way that you would like to be treated. No one has the right to pressure you. And you don't have the right to pressure anyone else. You should expect to be accepted, but you should also be accepting of others as well.

Always try to be a good friend. Supporting others is what being a true friend is really about. Pressuring them into doing things they don't want to do is not!

Put yourself in other people's places. If what you're doing to them would make you uncomfortable, don't do it.

It can be hard to deal with someone who has different opinions than you and who makes different decisions. Maybe you like to ride your bike without a helmet. You think wearing helmets isn't necessary and makes you look stupid.

If you're in trouble or feeling overwhelmed, don't be afraid to talk to an adult that you trust. Adults can offer advice to help you get through any tough times.

When you invite a friend to ride bikes, your friend brings along a helmet. Should you tease her for wearing a helmet? The answer is obviously no. You don't want to make her feel uncomfortable and unsafe. In fact, you could learn something from her; you should always wear your helmet when riding a bike! And in many places, you're breaking the law if you don't.

You should at least respect her decision. You should know that she gets to decide what to do in her own life. If you were her, that's what you would want to happen.

REACHING OUT

If you're having trouble with peer pressure, get help! You can talk to other people about it. They'll be able to help you and make you feel less alone.

You can talk to a good friend (someone who never pressures you). He has probably felt the same way you have before. Friends can comfort you. They can give you sympathy and support. But they can't always tell you what to do.

Talk to adults too. If you do not feel comfortable going to your parents with a problem, ask another trusted adult. You may not agree with her view on things, but just reaching out to someone

Get involved! You can use what you've learned from your own experiences to help others who might be having the same problem.

can help you work out the problem for yourself. At school, you can talk to teachers, guidance counselors, and school psychologists. They can all help you figure out how to deal with peer pressure. They might have the answers you are looking for. And they will definitely be willing to listen to your problems.

Adults may not completely understand your situation. But almost all of them have experienced peer pressure themselves at one time or another.

LISTEN TO GOOD ADVICE

Many young people have spoken out about negative peer pressure. They have good advice for other kids and teens dealing with peer pressure.

Danielle Wire, a high school student who was interviewed about an antidrug campaign, had some good advice. She says, "I try to deal with peer pressure by having a great support system." Her support system is made up of family and friends who encourage her to make good decisions and don't pressure her to make bad ones.

She goes on to say, "The thought of disappointing my friends and family **motivates** me to

Try to surround yourself with people who have the same goals and values that you do. That way, instead of pressuring each other to do something you don't want to do, you'll help each other be better!

Peer Pressure & Relationships

make the right decision. In the moment I stay calm, think things through, and make the right decision. I try to give a confident response that lets people know my values. Soon people realize how serious I am about my views and stop putting pressure on me." She pays attention to the good peer pressure her friends put on her to make the right decisions.

Another young person, McKenzie Batten, also depends on the support of friends. "I surround myself with good people that have the same values and are as motivated as I am," McKenzie said. "I usually don't have a problem with peer pressure, because I have amazing friends that are very supportive of me and we take care of each other."

A young man named Anthony Wonsono in Shanghai, China, had even more to say. He wrote a column for *Talk Magazine* (shanghai.talkmagazines.cn/issue/2011-04/youth-talk-coping-peer-pressure) about peer pressure. Anthony writes, "It is hard to say no. It is hard to say no to the temptations of life in Shanghai, to the friends you associate with, and to your rebellious nature."

Anthony hasn't given in to peer pressure. He doesn't make the same decisions some of his friends do. And he feels okay with his decisions! Anthony writes, "I have friends who smoke, club, and drink, yet they're still my friends, and I value them. Nonetheless, I don't need to agree with their actions, nor partake in them. In fact, a strong, non-wavering character should garner some respect."

He gives a list of facts that back up his decisions. He knows some of the things his friends do are really dangerous. So he has learned just how dangerous they are. Here are his facts, from the Adolescent Teen Services organization:

- A child who reaches age 21 without smoking, abusing alcohol, or using drugs is virtually certain never to do so.
- Teens that begin drinking before age 15 are five times more likely to develop alcohol dependence than those who begin drinking at age 21.
- It has been estimated that over three million teenagers are out-and-out alcoholics. Several million more have a serious drinking problem that they cannot manage on their own.
- The three leading causes of death for 15 to 24 year olds are automobile crashes, homicides, and suicides—alcohol is a leading factor in all three.
- Those **blasé** to drinking, drugs and partying may overlook these **statistics**, but these statistics act as warnings to those who say yes as well as those who say no. Mental limitations, alcohol dependence, emotional and psychological drawbacks, and the ever-present risk of death should never be taken lightly. Wouldn't you pay attention to the warnings of an earthquake and take shelter?

Anthony knows it's hard to say no. Young people want to say yes. He knows "they want to indulge and they want to fit in. Sometimes they believe that drinking and taking drugs will aid their social outlook; however this is where we must choose to be mentally strong."

He's writing to convince other young people not to give in. "We can limit ourselves and practice **restraint**. We can, but often, we don't. It is simply easier to say yes. I say no. How about you?"

What Can You Do to Stay Safe?

If you're having trouble, reach out to friends or family who can help you. Remember, you're not alone!

Peer Pressure & Relationships

Everybody deals with peer pressure. Sometimes when you're being pressured, it can seem like you're all alone. Everyone else is okay doing things like drinking, cheating on homework, and stealing. You're just the "uncool" one who isn't.

You might seem all alone, but you're definitely not. Lots of the people doing those things don't really want to. Peer pressure is something just about everyone has to deal with.

But that doesn't mean we have to accept it and give in! Learn how to deal with peer pressure and fight back. Feel free to be you!

Find Out More

ONLINE

Positive Peer Pressure
www.theemotionmachine.com/positive-peer-pressure

How to Cope with Peer Pressure
www.wikihow.com/Cope-with-Peer-Pressure

Dealing with Peer Pressure
www.kidshealth.org/kid/feeling/friend/peer_pressure.html

Peer Pressure
www.kidshelp.com.au/teens/get-info/hot-topics/peer-pressure.php

Respectful Relationships
www.kidshelp.com.au/grownups/news-research/hot-topics/respectful-relationships.php

IN BOOKS

Clark, Kate Stevenson. *Handling Peer Pressure (Character Education)*. New York: Chelsea House Publications, 2009.

Katz, Orly. *Peer Pressure vs. True Friendship: Surviving Primary School*. New York: Amazon Digital Services, Inc., 2013.

Raum. Elizabeth. *Tough Topics: Peer Pressure*. Portsmouth, N.H.: Heinemann, 2008.

Rechner, Amy. *The In Crowd: Dealing With Peer Pressure*. North Mankato, Minn.: Compass Point Books, 2009.

Schab, Lisa M. *Cool, Calm, and Confident: A Workbook to Help Kids Learn Assertiveness Skills*. Oakland, Calif.: Instant Help, 2009.

Index

About the Author & Consultant

Christie Marlowe was raised in New York City where she lives with her husband and works as a writer, journalist, and web designer.

Dr. Ronald D. Stephens currently serves as executive director of the National School Safety Center. His past experience includes service as a teacher, assistant superintendent, and school board member. Administrative experience includes serving as a chief school business officer, with responsibilities over school safety and security, and as vice president of Pepperdine University.

Dr. Stephens has conducted more than 1000 school security and safety site assessments throughout the United States. He was described by the *Denver Post* as "the nation's leading school crime prevention expert." Dr. Stephens serves as consultant and frequent speaker for school districts, law enforcement agencies and professional organizations worldwide. He is the author of numerous articles on school safety as well as the author of *School Safety: A Handbook for Violence Prevention*. His career is distinguished by military service. He is married and has three children.

Picture Credits